# Morning

# After

# Mourning

## By Elgina
## Bullock-Smith

BK
ROYSTON
Publishing

BK Royston Publishing
P. O. Box 4321
Jeffersonville, IN 47131
502-802-5385
http://www.bkroystonpublishing.com
bkroystonpublishing@gmail.com

Cover Design Photo: Elgina Bullock-Smith
Cover Design Layout: Elite Book Covers
Back Cover Family Photo: Ty Lockhart
Photography
Co-Editor: Lariah Spencer

ISBN-13: 978-1-951941-37-6

Printed in the United States of America

# Dedication

This book is dedicated to both my Anthony's fate and also I have decided that the honor will be bestowed upon my loving husband, Anthony Smith, Sr.

My love, just wanted you to know that I am okay. If you never read one line of this book because we've lived through this nightmare together, I can't say thank you enough for every prayer you covered me with, each healing hug you wrapped me in with your warm embrace, down to all the sleepless nights you stayed up with me making sure I didn't drown in my tears as I buried my face in your chest.

Babe, you're more than my husband, you are my soul mate.

# Table Of Contents

# Introduction

We all have heard of the grim reaper in many stories, films, and movies. But to actually have an encounter with his thieving presence, you're never prepared. Just fathom him in the same room with you, his dark shadow coming near, you knowing he can turn life into a lifeless one with one rigor mortis touch. Those that have felt the aftermath of his destruction, knows exactly what I'm talking about. You feel as if the reaper cashed in on his Groupon, the two for one special, at death's dinner. The only thing is you never knew your loved one had a reservation. Well, now that I think back over everything, I keep having this flashback memory that started way before AJ was even born.

I remember having this repeated nightmare. It started when I was about five months pregnant. I had just found out the sex of my unborn baby.

After giving him his father's name before birth, I couldn't wait to start shaping his personality. I felt Anthony was such as strong name for such a little baby. So, Anthony Sr. agreed that he too was given the nickname, Tony, as a small child. He and I pondered over TJ or AJ. I won the debate pointing out he's a junior and legally Anthony was his full name.

He paused and said, "AJ, huh?" In that very moment, I received a kick of confirmation as if the little guy in my tummy approved on his forever nickname. I began that day forming the bond of the mama's boy.

# Building The Bond

I would read, sing and just talk to him as if we had already met. I knew I was in love and that I needed to secure his love for me starting in the womb.

I had prayed to God after finding out I was with child and that I would have a healthy baby boy. I was so happy to see my prayer answered holding the Sonogram pictures proudly in my hands. It read Boy, pointing to his male parts.

Settling on a name to me was truly amazing. I was a mother to be. Danielle, also known as Danny, was so excited to have a new baby coming.

After she found out it was a brother, she was super happy.

I was so elated to have everyone's support. It was nice to know baby AJ was anxiously awaited. AJ would be the first grandchild for both my parents and the baby on his dad's side. Needless to say, there was plenty of aunts, uncles, cousins, and friends all signing up for babysitting passes. I remember the first time I had the nightmare. I passed it of as me eating too late before bed but, the way I recalled every detail stuck with me. I still can see what I know now was the hospital surgery room.

I remember feeling like it was me laying on the bed and the brightness from the overhead lights blinded me from seeing the face of the doctor who was pointing to me asking me in a frantic voice, "Do you still want to go through with this?"

I never answered him. I always jumped up out of my sleep with my heart racing a mile a minute but, my little bundle of joy would ensure me he was right there to comfort me and that allowed me to rest peacefully.

# Security Blanket

This dream happened once more right before my due date I was so close to having the baby my family started to have rotating members stay with me around the clock. This particular night was Tony's turn. He spent the night with me. We talked and he held my stomach feeling for himself our lives we're changing.

Coming to grips with the fact that he would have a daughter and a son. Giving me the gift of life, I'd be a first-time mother thanks to him. I had no problem falling asleep that night knowing I had both my

Anthony's with me. But the same recurring bully forced his way into my happy place, it was the same scene as if someone had hit the pause button on the remote.

I was back in the hospital room, this time I was standing at the door and not on the bed. I was still blinded from the brightness from the overhead light but, this time I saw the silhouette of a young man's body I had no idea who it was the doctor again turned to me frantically saying over and over do you still want him, can you handle it.

This time I reacted, I tried to run closer to see who this was and try to lend aid. I remember being held back being told no not to come any closer. So, without seeing the face I said yes, I do I still want him, him who I now know you AJ! My nightmare had become my reality.

# Umbilical Cord Love

No. Not my sweetheart. Not the mama's boy who always had to have me near him. I remember him as an infant, he would hold my finger and look straight into my eyes while I was nursing him. AJ had such a loving spirit and he was such a little lady's man. He even had this ear fetish where he would climb up on your lap and start rubbing your ears. Before he could even talk he'd just look at you, smile, and grab your earlobes. He would genuinely enjoy the texture that he felt, and it would soothe him right to sleep like the work of a pacifier. He did this for years all the way up to the 1st grade.

When He met new people, his opening statement was, "Hi, my name is AJ and I like ears." At this point, he had preferences of different ear types. He would sometimes say, "Mommy, I love your ears, they're so soft."

He would literally walk right up to people, catching them off guard, and say I like ears and begin rubbing their earlobe. We had to correct that behavior quickly before it offended anybody, but for the most part, close friends and family didn't mind it at all.

# The Charmer

I remember his first day of school and getting him, all dressed up as if it was picture day. I can still visualize his precious little face staring at me inhaling my every word. We had a morning prayer that I taught him at an early age and we would say it together every morning.

"Dear God, let me have a nice day. Let the teachers and the students be nice to me in every way. Father let me make it to school and back home safely each day. In Jesus' name, I pray,", and before I could end with Amen, AJ would shout it out, "Amen mommy", and give me the biggest smile, hug, and kiss. My heart melted every morning at 8:05 am.

I would say to him, "I'll be right here AJ when you get out of school buddy. Have a great big boy day Mommy loves you!" Once he was on the bus, he would always sit in the window seat so I could wave to him as he rode away out of my sight. Boy oh boy, the first goodbye almost killed me. It was so hard for me to trust someone with my heart being that he was my only child, and for the most part, my everything.

I wanted to spend every minute with him but, I knew I had taught him everything he needed to know as a 4-

year-old kid. The one thing I couldn't give him was relationship skills with people his own age.

That's the part that he'd have to figure out by himself. And so, would I. I honestly believe that he did a great job because he was always a loyal friend. AJ loved people and people loved AJ.

He was always the head of his class and to me, he was like a little computer. He could store knowledge and recall it so fluently. In AJ's leisure time, he would even read the dictionary because he said that he wanted to know every word and what it meant.

By the age of 10, AJ had a library

of his own which was very impressive, if I have to say so myself. I remember him learning about the amendments in the sixth grade after he found out about human rights. He was hooked.

He used what he had learned to his advantage so much so that we named him The Great Debater. We just knew that he was headed to Harvard to become an attorney.

But there was another side to him that went under the radar for years his love and passion for music. He just couldn't get past the lyrics that had been put to a beat Old school, Gospel, Country and Rap you name it.

He was obsessed with sound and meaningful words.

# The Faith Test

I can vividly remember him getting his first drum set for Christmas and how he hugged his daddy so tight and repeated over and over, "Oh thank you, God. Oh, thank you, Daddy. Oh Lord, thank you, Jesus" as if he had known that God had granted him with his heart's desires.

As a father, it brought Tony pleasure to see his child truly happy. That is actually brought him to tears of joy. That day, AJ's appreciation for his relationship with God and his dad encouraged my heart.

At that moment, I saw more than a

happy child. I saw the favor of God being displayed. I had no idea that Tony would pull this miracle off all by himself. I don't even know how he was able to get this past me.

I remembered us being out searching for a drum set and we couldn't find one that was in our price range. Honestly, they were all too expensive at the time, being that we were living on one income. Not to mention that I was then pregnant for the second time, with AJ's soon to meet little sister.

I didn't want to think about how we couldn't afford it or the fact we would have to scratch this off his most wanted list, but Christmas morning we all experienced the reward of having the precious gift of faith as AJ lovingly un-wrapped his gift.

AJ played them drums day in and day out. He had great rhythm, and natural talent.

# Lyrical Genius

Fast forward to around the age when AJ was in the 7th grade, he began writing some heavy poetry. He won all kinds of writing awards and earned distinguished titles on all of his writing assignments.

He began to use his love for words and music together by recording it all to the perfect beat. I can't say which one he worked harder on, mixing the right sound or creating the right lyrics but together it was a masterpiece.

He truly had something to say and an audience that wanted to hear it. As his mother, I was impressed and concerned at the same time because of his imagination it was so realistic that you could really get drawn in visually.

AJ began to become quite popular as he was becoming known for more than being one of the smartest kids in class. He was now the cool kid too.

# Morally Ground It

My husband Anthony Sr. and I noticed the difference in the number of friends Anthony Jr. was beginning to bring over to the house. By the time AJ hit sixteen Permit driving age I wasn't comfortable not knowing the backstory of the company he was keeping so for liability purposes I've always managed to basically pre-screen all his grade school friends.

I knew their Moms, Dads, and any participating family members' names and phone numbers before we ever exchanged kids for play dates. Just for insurance.

However, AJ's new group of friends really didn't have much of a support system. He would bring people home for dinner all the time and sometimes I'd catch him taking two and three extra snacks out of the house at a time.

I wouldn't say anything, I would just watch him go out the back door, around to the side of the house, and pass out the food as if he was on a resource mission of some sort. I had mixed emotions, but for the most part, I was truly grateful that he had a giving heart.

AJ played outside with the boys through dinnertime most nights, so I waited for him in the kitchen one night until he came in for curfew I sit with him quietly at the kitchen table while he ate his dinner.

I moved closer to sit beside him thinking to myself right before he clears his plate I'm going to ask him about taking so many snacks from the pantry. It was my cue so I asked?

He proceeds to talk to me about his friends and their personal situations. He looked me right in the eye and said, "Mom, I'm sorry. I just couldn't eat in their face knowing that they were hungry too, so I had to share with them."

I couldn't say or do anything but nod my head with approval and grab his hand. I explained that his dad and I were very proud of him and I patted him on his head fully understanding his position in the matter. I finished our conversation for the night replying son You did right by sharing.

# Sharing Is Caring

From that day on, our grocery bill skyrocketed. Suddenly, AJ had a full Haven house going on. Each child had a situation worse than the other it seemed like.

I quickly began to see first-hand that there was truly a need for a youth ministry. Those young men were homeless hungry and looking for an idol, which was all the perfect plot for the devil's workshop.

# Bonus Babies

I began to form my own relationship with the boys, asking surface questions just to get an idea of their background. Some would just simply answer me with a short reply, Yeah or Nah, while others had basic manners, ending their statements with yes ma'am or no ma'am.

I knew I had to be a mother figure for all of them because they affectionately called me Mama Gina. So that sealed the deal, all the boys loved my cooking.

They all knew that I had 3 rules when visiting the Smith house:

1. Be respectful,

2. No profanity, that I could hear at least and,

3. Wash those dirty hands before you touch my food.

# Round Table Discussion

I loved watching the boys eating and enjoyed the warmth of our little family setting. I would sometimes enter the kitchen interrupting their rap session. It seemed like they never minded my presence; they were so happy to see me and I was equally glad to see them.

I would always ask them about their day and all current events happening in their lives. They would update me and then thank me for the meal I had prepared for them to demolish.

Sometimes after they would eat

they would ask me, "Mama Gina you need anything done around the house?" Those boys were eager to lend a helping hand. I guess as a kind repayment gesture for my loving hospitality, they could be so sweet. Most of the time they would help AJ with his chores as if they were really his brothers. Thinking back, that's exactly what they were to him.

# Two For One

AJ always wanted a brother and when he found out that I was expecting a baby, he asked if it was going to be a boy. I remember when I broke the news to him that he was getting a baby sister.

AJ looked at my protruding belly and said, "That's ok I will love her too. You can just have me a baby brother next time." I just smiled somehow knowing that there wasn't going to be the next time, I just didn't have the heart to tell him.

When his little sister finally arrived, we named her Lanyia. Boy,

He loved her so much that he called her "his baby." From birth, AJ cared for her and protected her. As he shifted from being the baby to now being the "middle-child," sandwiched in between two sisters, he was finally older than someone else.

He thought that he was now the boss. Their sibling bond was unbelievably close. However, he longed for male companions and the boys fulfilled that for him forming the best of both worlds.

AJ was the perfect mixture of truth and loyalty he really was the glue that held everyone together.

# Middle Child Male Advantageous

AJ had it made being positioned in between an older and younger sister, he was able to be led by one sister and was able to pass down and teach the baby sister. I can remember countless times Danielle and AJ plotting for ambushed on my husband and I. From her coaching AJ into asking for the company to stay over for the night, on down to her becoming a mother dropping the grandchildren off without us being informed.

AJ would agree to babysit for a small sitter's fee; however, after about an hour of him hiding he was working a babysitting gig, out would always pop one of the grands, "GMama I'm hungry."

To my surprise, I would reply, "How did you all get here?" looking right into their Precious Eyes.

"My mommy," they replied and at that moment I knew we had been set up. Those two got us like that all the time. AJ got paid and we got played. They were thick as thieves. They've always kept each other's secrets and acted as bodyguards for one another. their relationship was sacred. Nyia even struggled to gain entrance into their brother's sister circle by her being the baby made her the weaker link she was loved but not trusted.

They tested her on several missions and into their demise, she failed with flying colors every time. So, they began to just use her as bait for their hook strategizing the master plan.

# Us Against Them

However, what they didn't know was we were on to them. Nyia was a human 'truth detector' she couldn't lie to save her soul. You know, sweet and innocent, she was easy to decode.

With her help, we sunk their battleship many days from her leads. We would corner her in the kitchen close to the snack pantry and say these 3 words, 'want a snack?' Boy, it was just that simple. "Yes ma'am," she'd reply. "ok," I'd say, "pick yourself something out."

She'd go from shelve to shelve scanning over the perfect goody for her tummy. After she took, possession we swarmed around her like a car dealer trying to seal the deal.

Have a quick set down we want to just ask a few questions before you leave. By this time, the duo knew we had a good idea something was suspicious. Nyia would lay out the details like putting a piece to a jigsaw puzzle. We would say ok baby you can take your snack to your room now and don't tell your sister and brother about our snack secret or you can't have anymore. Knowing this was the only way to keep the dogs off our tracks we stayed clear and let Nyia become our little middle man and a good one at that she was.

# The Rebound Buddy

Years later, after Danielle was old enough to move out on her own, it was hard for AJ to do his magic without his assistant, so he had to trust and train Nyia. She would lovingly cook for him, help him with chores and even pick us.

For him, the table had turned in his favor. He had a new sidekick they would do everything together. Life was good for them both.

They explored a relationship they never knew way possible. Nyia was no longer the baby brat and AJ was no longer the big brother bully. They were synchronized siblings. He loved her and she respected him, and we loved their bonds and wouldn't have ever dreamed it would be broken between the three.

# What A Difference A Day Makes

My family's journey into this new normal started roughly on February 7, 2015. Life as I knew it and somehow took for granted suddenly ended with a horrible feeling that began when a phone call went unanswered. As I look back over that spring-like February morning, it started like most weekends that we shared in the Smith household.

We all got up and started moving around and going about our day with a pre-planned schedule that included a weekend to-do list. However, this particular weekend, it was our grandson, Daniel's birthday party. I got up early to ensure that my errands and my time that day would line-up.

As I was heading to the bathroom for my morning shower my phone rang and it was the oldest child of our three children and Daniel's mother, Danielle. "Well good morning", she said extra perky, "I'm calling to remind you guys about this evening." I replied out loud, "Don't forget to bring socks, okay, we're meeting at 6:00 pm, at Sky Zone Got it? See you later."

From the corner of my eye, I felt my husband hanging on to the thoughts of my last statement. So, there was no need to relay the message. My husband looked at me with confirmation that he had overheard the entire conversation.

I began to restart my morning rituals and my first target was the bathroom. I quickly realized that I needed to leave the bathroom door cracked as I started my hot water for my sauna-like shower, leaving room for the hot steam to have an escape route.

I had just styled my hair the night before and I had no time for natural hair do-overs. While lathering my tired body, I began to think to myself, this to-do-list is a mile long. I began to mentally rehearse my day's plan of action. At 10:00, I have to be at the church, then I'll go to the grocery store, which is near Danielle and there's a copy store near there too."

Boy, I had the day planned to the minute. As I ended my shower, I turned the knobs and could hear a conversation between my husband and AJ. I grabbed and fumbled with my robe making sure I was decent before I opened the restroom door to go finish up my business in my bedroom.

From the hallway, I could still hear my husband in the kitchen talking to AJ about the birthday party for Daniel. I heard My husband say to him, "Hey man, you are coming to the party today." AJ replied, "Huh? Nah. I'm tired daddy."

Finishing his argument with, "I worked late last night and then stayed up way too late with Coby. I'm sleepy so I'm just going to get him a gift." I paused from entering my bedroom door when I heard his response and as his mother, I shouted out to him from the hallway, "Anthony Jerome Smith Jr." calling him by his whole government name, "You know you need to go to your nephew's birthday party."

I continued walking into my room feeling disappointed. As I sat down in front of my vintage vanity I finished up my makeup in the mirror and never placed eyes on his face just exchanged sound. He knew from the tone in my voice that I didn't want him to stay home.

# The Biggest Regret Of My Life

Right now, to this very day, I truly wish I had pushed harder to make him go anyway. Sadly, he didn't attend. My husband, daughter, and I, all left the house and got into the car to start off what I planned to be a fun-filled day.

# The Turn Of Events

If my memory serves me right, we hadn't even been gone away from the house 3 hours running our errands for the day before I got a call from one of my close friends.

I answered, "Hey girl, what's up?" She said, in a peculiar firm voice, "What's going on over your house?"

I replied with a question for her, "I don't know, why?"

Almost too nervous to ask, I quickly said, "What's wrong? I'm not there." She paused for what felt like an hour.

She took a deep breath and said,

"Well you need to get home."

I replied, "Ok, do you know why?"

She hesitated once more to the point that I felt that the call may have dropped. I said, "Hello...Hello...are you still there?"

She said, "Gina, you have yellow tape surrounding your house and there're dogs and cops all in your front yard."

# Panic Mold

My heart dropped instantly. All I could think to do was drop everything that I had in my hands and run. I ran like an Olympic runner back to the car where my husband and daughter were waiting for me.

After the last 3 stores of my seek and find assignment sheet, they had decided to stop playing with me and stayed this round in the car.

From a distance, I made eye contact with them.

My husband began to anxiously cheer me on, "Come on baby. Run baby. RUN!" As I got closer to the truck, he saw the stress in my eyes as I began to call out orders like a diner cook, "Nyia, call Nana. I'm calling AJ and Babe just drive, we need to get home!"

I noticed out of my peripheral that no one moved. They literally wanted more information and right at that moment, I had no time to explain.

I kept calling AJ's phone but when I didn't get an answer, I kept redialing it over and over.

# Searching For Answers

I heard Nyia say, "Hello Nana. Are you ok? Alright. Are you on your way home?"

She shared that information out loud so I could get her confirmation of her calling.

My husband had started driving and then asked me again, "Babe, what's wrong?"

I said, "I just got a call that we needed to get home. I was told that the cops are at our house with the K9 dogs, and they have our house roped off with yellow tape."

He put his feet on the gas pedal like

an Indy 500 race car driver. We got from one end of town to the other in record timing.

# Where Are You?

I was still dialing AJ's number with no answer. This worried me deeply because he had NOT answered my calls. Generally, if he missed the first call, he quickly interrupted my second attempt with a return call back.

Frantically and coincidently, we all made it home within seconds of each other. We pulled up to the house as close as we could since the police had stopped traffic everywhere on my normally quiet street.

People were all out of their neighborhood businesses and residents gathering around like an episode from the movie zombies. I felt they were all heading in our direction but luckily, they were intercepted by the Louisville Metro Police.

# The Silent Treatment

I spotted the first approachable police officer and asked, "Excuse me, sir. I live here. Can you please tell me what's going on?"

He said, "This is a crime scene to a triple homicide."

His stern voice carried over the crowds' noise when he asked, "Can you tell me who all lives here with you?"

I began to do a physical roll call and as I started with myself, then saying, "here comes my husband."

As he walked over with my daughter I introduced the rest of them,

"That's our daughter, Lanyia, and she's my mother, Jeanine."

Explaining our 18-year-old son AJ, Anthony Jr, is the only member not present. I instantly started feeling like I was going into a panic attack.

The officer said, "Do you have a current picture of AJ?"

We all said, "Yes!" I couldn't get my phone to unlock and it was like my mind couldn't decode what all was happening.

Lanyia was first to hand over her device to the officer, showing him one of AJ's latest Instagram famous photos she had taken for him. The officer took a glance and passed the phone to another officer and stated to us, "You all will not be able to re-enter the house." Something about them ordering to have a search warrant.

Dumb confused, we all looked at the officer and said together, like a group of copy cats, "Why? What is the reason?"

He seemed to ignore the question and said some fancy police mumbo-jumbo into his walkie-talkie and had us suddenly escorted across the street to be taken to wait in a parked cop car. They eventually told us that until the investigation was done, we had to remain away from the house.

# Sound The Alarm

We had so many questions and no one would answer us. I tried to occupy my mind by making calls to local family members, trying not to alarm them, but to ask if anyone had heard from or seen AJ, in the past couple of hours.

Well, that didn't go so well since my brother and sister in love could hear in my voice that something didn't sound right. They insisted that they were on their way to my house.

That meant that they would soon see it was more than I lead on. I kept calling AJ in between the other contacts. I placed calls to his friends and nearby neighbors, but no one answered, or they said that they were not at home themselves.

# Where Is My Child?

The hours were passing by way too quickly without any updates. My sister in love – Iisha convinced me to start calling around to the nearby hospitals. I made 1 call and couldn't talk or remember what to even say so I quickly appointed her over that task.

My focus was on calling my son and hopefully hearing his voice reply, "Mom, I'm ok." But instead, I continued to call, and each time I repeated out loud, "AJ come on. Pick up…pick up…PICK UP YOUR PHONE!"

Right in the middle of my ranting,

I get a tap on my shoulder with a look that I will never forget.

Iisha said, "Gina, the lady from University Hospital wants to talk to you."

My mind instantly took me on a jaw-dropping rollercoaster ride. These are the words I now have painted like graffiti on my memory wall, "Yes hello, we have a person here with the name Anthony Smith here in the hospital. We have been looking for his next to kin, there aren't any family members present. This individual has been here for several hours now. We are going to need you to come up here if you want more information. That's all I can share over the phone."

She ended with, "Hurry but drive safe." I kept replaying, hurry, hurry, thinking hurry doesn't sound good at all.

# What Are You Trying To Tell Me?

I jumped out of the cop cruiser and met my silent practicing husband at the curb. He had exited the car some time ago to make his own phone calls and clear his thought pattern.

I knew he was truly trying to remain hopeful thinking that this was all a mistake of identity and nothing was wrong. I looked him in the face with teardrops collecting in the corners of my eyes.

I slowly grabbed for his embrace and said, "We called the hospital babe. They think they have AJ there." He stepped back with dismay and then blurted out like air leaving a balloon, "I don't believe he's there I'm staying here. You all can go. I'm not leaving from in front of this house. I'm waiting for AJ to come home."

Wow, those words punched me like a heavyweight boxer. If you were to know the character behind my husband's demeanor, this was very out of the ordinary for him to be quick, blunt, rude, and snappy with anyone, especially me, his wife, tears were now falling down my face uncontrollably. I decided to respect his request and leave with permission granted from the nonchalant officer, we all headed out to the hospital.

I can still see the look of relief on

the face of that officer. His rosy cheeks looked like he had been forced to keep a terrible tasting secret that he wanted to spit out. An awful shocking secret that would soon be revealed to us.

# Take Me To Him

We arrived at the hospital at exactly 8:17 pm. It seemed that my memory wanted this moment captured and framed mentally for reasons beyond me.

Once checking in at the hospital, we were quickly greeted with, "You're the Smith family? Ok. Who's the mother of Anthony?"

I sat down at the admissions desk taking ownership that I had a missing son. The clerk started pushing pens and release forms to be signed, then in a split second, up pops a priest and detectives, all needing my attention, simultaneously.

I finally said, "Wait!"

In a louder than my regular indoor speaking voice but trying not to come undone or cause a scene, reminding myself, you don't even know if it's even AJ that they have here so, stay calm.

Well, that lasted about 1 minute when the detective started making away for my escape. He escorted us to a private, dim room to safely break the news that would shatter my family's life to the core forever.

The awkward movements in the room went like a scene from a TV court show. We were told to take a seat and not to open the door or answer our phones. We were all puzzled with fear of what was to come from his mouth.

The Chaplin stood closer to me but near the door. I strangely remember the fresh smell of cleaner from the freshly mopped floor being detailed on the other side of the door in the hallway.

My mind wanted out of that room, so I took whatever avenue I could get. The detective saw that I was trying to escape so he began handcuffing my thoughts, he called my name, "Elgina, that's how you pronounce your name right?"

I glanced over to him and replied, "Yes. That's right."

He said, "Well, we have 3 young men here and 2 of them are still in surgery and well."

Well, what! I yelled from on the inside of myself. I couldn't take it anymore, I said, "Well what sir?"

Trying to mentally solve his seek and find, He paged the surgeon who I would soon discover had worked on our beloved AJ.

# It Wasn't What I Wanted To Hear

The doctor came into the room quietly and sat down next to the detective and began to ask for descriptive details about AJ. He introduced himself with, "I'm head of surgery here at the hospital and I'm here to ask a few critical questions to help identify your family member."

"Mom, is it?" he said looking right at me, "Can you tell me what he looks like or better yet does he have any tattoos?"

I answered slowly, "Yes he has a tattoo." I quickly recalled the ugly truth behind the cover-up tattoo. I described that he had one on the upper right side of his chest.

It was a crown that once spelled my name. He had gotten it done from an entry-level tattoo artist who butchered my name up so bad in bubble letters. AJ was ashamed to ever reveal it on a daily basis which is why he never went shirtless.

He begged us to help pay for it to get fixed or covered up so for his 16th birthday gift, we had it covered with a crown he was so happy with his new cooler professional ink job. After the patch up he stayed shirtless.

Who would have ever thought this would define our fate?

The doctor proceeded by saying,

"The person believing to be your son, the one with the crown on the upper chest area took the brunt of the whole ordeal."

My brother Jr. said, The whole ordeal? What happened?"

# Don't You Dare Say It

"Well," he replied, "AJ was shot in the chest."

We all gasped for breath and before we could even finish emptying our lungs like a drowning helpless swimmer, we were overtaken by what was the tide of his massive wipe out by the sentence.

"Yes, he suffered 2 gunshots wounds. The one to the chest wasn't the injury that ended his life. Your son, AJ, Anthony Jr. died at 7:55 this evening from the gunshot wound he suffered to his head."

# I Hate It Here

We all collapsed right where we were as if we were playing a game of freeze tag. The whole room went silent. I felt life leaving my body. I knew as I laid on that cold hospital floor, crying uncontrollably that I had just sat through my own funeral. A part of me just died from that information.

# Life Is But A Vapor

I wasn't that fun loving, outgoing Gina anymore. She had flat lined and her remains were in the morgue next to her baby boy, AJ. I literally heard my spirit talking, "Elgina, no, don't do this. You can't leave Nyia. She is going to need her mother."

I kept holding on to the easy route out, not taking another breathe, that way I knew death would come and finish me off. It would be as if I died from a broken heart which wouldn't be a lie.

# The Rude Awakening

But my heart kept racing and wouldn't let me leave. I took one look over where Nyia was laying all spread out over the wall, like her spine had been broken in half, she was just limp. My spirit said, "Look at your baby. She's just lost her brother and now you're going to leave her too. Please Gina, don't do this to your family."

I wasn't sure what to do, but I knew if I inhaled another ounce of oxygen this would be my truth. According to what I was just told, our son, my first love, AJ had died, alone in the hospital. The same exact place where he was born, within the same hour but this time, without me.

I ached from the aftershocks that were repeatedly attacking my thinking that he's never even been to a doctor's visit without me. The fact that he died alone was more than I could allow myself to imagine.

I was fading in and out of consciousness.

Out of nowhere, this stranger came up to me and began screaming, "No! Wake up! Breathe! You have to breathe!" She started banging on my chest as if she were knocking on a door demanding for help. She huffed and puffed and almost blew my lights out permanently.

I was forced to regained consciousness due to her brutal beating. An elder, from our ministry, Pastor Sanchez, swatted her away like a pestering bug never to see her again. Thank the Lord he came to my aid.

I breathed in one large breath of air and unmuted my background. Everyone was talking and crying and relieved that I was now responding.

In rushed several nurses and staff with oxygen and a gurney. They counted, 1…2…3 as they transferred me to the gurney.

They quickly had me strapped to the bed and headed to the emergency room, where they had already taken my mother fearing she could've been experiencing a heart attack.

# Snapped

I screamed as if I were being kidnapped. "No! Help me! Let me go! I want to see my son!" I was in such a rage that I somehow broke free from the bed, sat up and demanded that they take me to my AJ. Everyone was in shock that my recently lame body had so much strength that I physically destroyed a hospital bed.

Church members, hospital staff and family began to try to calm me down. They finally reasoned with me that after I settled down, they could see if I could be with AJ. So, I tried so hard to regain my composure, however, my husband who finally decided to come to the hospital, heard my voice and not knowing the verdict ran to my aid my wailing cry.

"Babe?" He says, while clearing a path through the crowded hallway, rushing to find out what's wrong with me. I started screaming for him, knowing my knight in shining armor would help me.

"They won't let me see him."

He replied, "See who?"

I shouted, "AJ! He's by himself. He died by himself babe!"

# He Lost Too

My husband's knees buckled, and these words followed as he hit the concrete floor, "The sins of the father fall onto the son."

I had heard that before but, couldn't place the dialogue in that moment. However, at this point, I had more time than he did to process this information. So, I held him with one arm and my bleeding heart with the other.

I couldn't take it anymore. I had to get out of here. The smell from the freshly mopped floor that once caught my attention, now held me prisoner and I needed to be freed. I wanted to run as far away as I could from this nightmare that we were in.

I hated leaving my baby there but, I had no choice. All of our parental rights were revoked. My sorrow was causing me to act out of character. The detective, the coroner and the priest, all repeatedly told me that I didn't want to see him in this present condition, please go and get some fresh air and some rest.

# Don't Tell Me How To Feel

I couldn't find anything refreshing about breathing in air that was now cut off from my child. And not to mention rest. Rest where? My house was now included in an investigation, and I still had no idea why or knowledge of what happened to my son that lead us to this uncharted path of preparing to plan a funeral. No one could ever coach us through what we had to face next.

# Not Now Please

The news reporters, the spectators and those misleading policemen were all a part of our frequent reminders that AJ is now gone.

There wasn't a place or person that we could turn to without questions. Our whole lives were being dissected under a microscope. Every time we turned on the television, we saw AJ's face.

We were being followed and harassed by the local news station because all they wanted was coverage for the 6 o'clock news. But to us, this was our reality and we didn't want to discuss it or live it out on TV.

# Invaded

All we really did was mourn and process this brutal truth. We had no idea when AJ's body would be released to us. His body was being processed, labeled and tagged as evidence, like a particle found in a crime scene investigation. He couldn't be released to us until the investigation was over.

Planning and prayer was all we could do during the first week. On a Wednesday morning, I remember getting a phone call out of nowhere from an unfamiliar number that I couldn't recall and wasn't in my recorded phone log as a person I knew.

The call didn't even match any of the numbers from the stack that I had collected from the police and news reporters. So, I answered with reservations not knowing who was on the other end. I took a deep breath quickly thinking of a response to this caller's ploy.

To my surprise, a sweet and fragile voice spoke into my ear. "Hello. Is this Mrs. Smith?"

Using my best customer service voice, I replied, "Yes. Yes, it is. How may I help you?"

"Hello. I'm from hospice and I received your information to reach out to you and your family to inform you about our services." She went on to say, "We aid in support for families like yours." I thought to myself, like mine? I was in shock that hospice made calls to homicide families. I climbed out of my thoughts and said, "Excuse me one moment but, may I ask, how did you get my number?" Her patient voice responded, "I received your contact information from the homicide department. They are the ones who submitted your number to us."

I sat up while listening and thinking to myself, 'the nosy detectives, and cops that had been knocking on our door day and night.'

She interpreted my thoughts once more following up with, "Yes, the homicide department is connected to our Hope and Healing program, so we work closely with them to assist families like yours with resources like counseling and even grief camp. Do you think this could be something your family would be in need of?" I couldn't believe my ears.

# The Smoke Signal

The very same people that I was angry with were trying to help my family. Before I allowed my hopes to be lifted, I said, "Ma'am. Are you 100% sure that you can help us? Our son was killed."

She answered, "I understand and yes, people who have experienced sudden death and homicide are who we help."

Because she couldn't see me, I felt safe to release the pressure building up in my tear ducts. I began to cry tears that flowed from a river of joy and let out a sigh of relief. Finally, someone with experience, who could honestly help us wanted to reach out to my family.

# No Clue On What To Do

During the next few days, we were told to find a funeral home that would receive AJ and prepare him for his home going service. This was the part that kept me up most nights, thinking and worrying how he would look.

Would I be able to recognize him? Facing the agony of the "what ifs" caused me to drop 15 pounds in a week. I was made to go to the doctor for sleep aids and mood stabilizer even though I didn't want any medication.

I had just totally lost my appetite for life. I wanted to starve this death thing right out of me. My mind mulled over all the needed logistics day in and day out. Being that I had only asked to plan pamper parties, baby showers and birthday parties, the weight of the perfect home going celebration was too much for me to handle alone. I had no idea where to have his body sent.

This was much different than asking my girlfriends to refer me to some great pediatrician or a nice after school program. I needed help with placing my most valuable gift into the hands that would ultimately handle all my child's final needs. Who…where…how would I get this done?

# When Death Comes To
# A Believer

For the first time in weeks, I felt I needed to fuel up my faith. I was running really low since missing Sunday service and weekly bible study.

Our church family members loved us by coming over daily with food, hugs and prayer. Praise Covenant Church never left our side. However, my soul was in pain and we needed a faith boost. I needed to get out of the house and step into the house of the Lord.

Although we didn't have service as normal, we were asked by the church if they could hold a special memorial service for our family and friends since we were still setting a funeral date.

# Faith Talk

Tony and I arrived at the memorial service late and to my surprise, it felt like the whole city packed themselves into this medium sized fellowship hall. As we were guided down the aisle by the usher to our front row seats. I took a mental photo of everyone's faces. There were so many people. Many were crying and others had pain in their eyes. It became very clear that yes, they were there to support us but honestly, they were all there for AJ.

Our son in some manner played a part in their lives as well. Having that memorial service was for most unselfish idea that we had agreed to in days. It was breathtaking to see the crowd of classmates, neighborhood friends, and co-workers who were there to openly grieve the loss of Anthony, Bone, J Real and our son, AJ.

This loving, talented, loyal person was someone very important to so many. As I looked around at all the people who had gathered in that one place, I began to process and even feel compassionate about their emotions.

The whole event took a turn for the greater good. We allowed God to use the common bond between all of us to unite us in peace, even if it was just for that setting that peace surpassed all of our understanding of that famous cliché (why) AJ. Instead, we said because of AJ, we now have to live differently for him and secure our spot in heaven to ensure that we will meet him again.

# Testifying

I was asked by my pastor to say a few words publicly to those who were in attendance. Tony and I stood there together in front of what felt like thousands of people. At first, I had nothing to say. I was mentally in this unfamiliar place of grasping the moment. I can still hear the clicks from the media's cameras as I began to have what I now realize as a holy boldness moment.

I looked right in the recording "red eye" of that camera lens like I was talking to Lucifer himself and said, "Satan, the body of Jesus is against you. You will not take another person in this room's life. I plead the blood over every person in this room." I then felt compelled to speak to his friends/brothers, also my bonus babies, that were in my vision's range.

I began to explain to them how precious they are to their families, us and most importantly to God, the creator. He desired a relationship with all of them. I also explained that to see AJ again, the key was to get in a relationship with God so he could save them from sin, and that getting reborn again was a fresh start to a better life.

My mind went back to AJ's dedication service that we had for him as a baby when he was just a few weeks old. My mother kept telling me about the importance of having your baby dedicated back to God, so we did. We stood in front of the church, holding our beloved bundle of joy dressed in all white. Some would call what he wore a christening outfit. My childhood pastor took AJ out of my arms and began anointing his little body with blessed olive oil.

I can still hear him say right before he handed him back to me, "The same God that giveth can taketh away."

I began to understand in that present moment what he meant by that back then.

# Facing Facts

Wow! It's crazy how your mind can go back and catch a memory in a sea full of other thoughts that occurred years ago. But to explain what happened next blows my mind.

I ended my statement with, "Come now while the blood is still running warm in your veins. Come renew your relationship with God. Please, if you care anything about me and my husband, please don't have us worried about where your souls would be if something were to happen to you."

I had never orchestrated an alter call before, but this is exactly what happened.

So many young people flooded the alter for prayer and to rededicate their lives back to God.

19 people were baptized that night. That gave my faith the best rejuvenation I could have ever asked for. I noticed even the news reporters that came to survey the evening got in the prayer line and soon the entire crew was told to wrap up. The anchor woman decided that we needed to continue in private, that was something we weren't expecting to hear.

# Ready Or Not

February 12th, two days before Valentine's Day, AJ's body was ready to be released to the funeral home of our choice. Again, being totally green in this area, I had no idea on where to go or what to expect. I was told by a close friend to just grab your insurance information and that they would sit in and help go over the final arrangements.

I thought, "Okay, I can do this. No problem."

Well, I went to retrieve my important documents I kept safely filed in a corner drawer. I fingered through them, searching for the policy with AJ's name on it. I suddenly remembered seeing a letter addressed to him with this same insurance company seal on the envelope from a few months back, opened and left for junk mail on the kitchen table.

I go right to where my mind leads me to match up the information, however, the policy was in my name, but this letter was addressed to him. It turns out that it was a cancellation letter advising me that his coverage would end under my name and that he would lose his spot as a child under my coverage. As I now held the letter in my hands, I remembered having this conversation and asking him what it was all about.

I began to slightly remember talking about it with AJ while preparing dinner one night.

We briefly talked about it and he did what he normally would do and simply replied, "I'll handle it later."

# Uninsured

As a matter of fact, his exact words while reading the documents were, "Nah, man. They trying to get all my money. I'll just get insurance from work for way cheaper."

I didn't press the issue and said, "Okay son, but you're going to need insurance AJ! You hear me?" Snapping out of that flashback, I sat down at the same kitchen table and had a whole conversation with myself.

How could I have allowed my 18-year old child to handle something so important like this? I saw where he had started the application and never completely filled it out. I ran back to my room to compare cancellation dates and even the fine print. I said to myself, 'Oh Lord, we don't have insurance for him! He's no longer covered.' It was like I was driving down the road and instantly caught a flat tire. Who's going to help you without roadside assistance? That's what insurance coverage was, in my opinion, in case of an emergency. Oh, and did we have an emergency!

"Jesus" is all I kept saying. "Oh Lord, no not this." I began to quote scripture. "You said in your word, you wouldn't put more on me than I could bare." My baby, who never even finished school or got married and had kids or grew up into old age with his sisters. "Oh, AJ!"

He needed my help, and in that moment, I was useless.

I averaged up all my parenting points and tallied up a failing grade on my overall mothering skills. "Elgina, how in the world are you going to fix this before Tony finds out? He's going to completely come undone from the embarrassment of not having the money or resources to bury his only son." I laid in a puddle of my tears, pleading with God for help.

The phone rings, I answered and heard the sweet voice of my dear friend, Wanda Holt. "Hey lady, you ready? I told the funeral home we'd be there by five." I couldn't break the news to her that my only assignment was undone.

All I was asked to do was gather the policy and write down the basic information about his life, birth place, our names, etc. I heard Tony blowing the horn and I walked out to meet him as he waited for me in the car.

I remained quiet the whole ride over. I'm assuming he thought I was sad about the planning taking place. We pulled up to the funeral home and I felt like I'm about to bust with guilt. I grabbed my husband's shoulder and said, "Wait. There's something I need to tell you before we go in there."

# The Truth Will Set You Free

He said slowly looking out the window, "Gina, they're waiting on us."

I said, "This can't wait." Blurting out, "AJ doesn't have any insurance. He was removed from our insurance policy back in October."

He looked at me and said, "What?" I lowered my head and repeated that he hasn't been covered.

"Now what?" wasn't his only reply but, it was his question to me regarding this new news.

"I don't know." We both grabbed for the door noticing our pastor, his wife and the funeral home coordinator were waiting for us at the door.

We take seats around this wooden round table where we were presented with books filled with colorful different textured caskets. They had big ones, little ones, blue ones and gold ones with words engraved on them. I felt so sick to my stomach that I had to be excused for a moment. My mind went on a scavenger hunt knowing my son's body was somewhere in this place.

# Soul-Searching

Having him sent there was the first process to prepare his body for the funeral. I almost became a burglar. I felt like I needed to break into one of the locked doors to receive my priceless keepsake that was stolen from me. But fear apprehended me, so I came back from the restroom tour and took my seat. Everyone looked at me to see if I was okay, my facial expressions answered all of the questions, 'No, I'm not okay at all.'

I sat there like I was being bitten from ants in my pants, I got so nervous from knowing the big question would be popped soon at any moment.

"Where is the policy?" The policy that would pay for all the things we needed to bury our child. I nodded as a form of agreement and had somehow selected in an imaginary shopping cart. After waiting for the sound of her calculator to stop tapping and tallying up the bill, she wrote down the figure and passed it over like we were attending a silent auction.

I knew in the back of my mind we lost whatever the bid was months ago with the lapsing of his policy. She asked us to look over it while we looked over the policy. I started to hand it to her but I said to myself, "She is going to find out one-way or another that this wasn't an even exchange."

'Elgina,' I coach myself, 'the truth is the light out of the world, so tell the truth.'

I said, "Ma'am earlier today I found out that Anthony, or AJ, doesn't have insurance anymore. He was dropped from our family policy as a child term rider back in October. I thought this policy was still active until I remembered the letter addressed to him back in the fall before the holidays. He told me that he will get insurance from work in that it will be deducted from his paycheck.

However, along with the cancellation letter his new insurance policy packet was never completed."

She took the paper with the total back and began to rewrite and deduct items from my imaginary shopping cart as if I were a shopper that took my window browsing a little overboard. She presented us with a much lower number that was still too high for our current weekly budget; however, at this point, it was what it was, business.

# Let the Marathon Begin

She firmly informed us of the following, "You have until the 13th to have his clothes, and money for the service needs to be in by the 15th. I don't handle money the day of the service. So, in order to keep your February 16th date, we need the body to be prepared and dressed by tomorrow because we aren't working on Valentine's Day. Again, all money will be due by the 15th before 5:00 p.m. Do you all understand? If not, we have no other choice but to have him sent back to the hospital where they will bury him for you for free without you. They don't provide services for the family."

Feeling the pain and push, I had never raced with the clock before but, somehow I knew we could do this with every tick and tock that mentally challenged me.

We we're literally competing with time. We both decided to go against all odds meaning by any means necessary. This was the last thing we as his parents were going to do for him, and we wanted to do it right. We called lawyers, banks, loan companies and even thought to sell off stuff. Well, a loan company called back and told us, sure we can lend you the money.

Angelic music to our ears. We

made the deadline with only minutes to spare.

# The Loss Legacy

The next couple of days, we all walked around on eggshells not really speaking, compartmentalized all that we had to do prior to attending AJ's viewing that would be taking place in a few hours.

The tension was so thick you could cut it with a knife Anthony, my husband, and I never fully talked about the facts and things that were playing in our own heads. You know the sneaky blame monster who wanted to catch us off guard and have his way with us, turning our union into an unfair game of UNO.

You know how the deck is stacked up against you and the other person just keeps making you draw and pick up cards of regret? I kept praying, "Lord keep my mind, my heart, my spirit, and my marriage." I noticed Anthony becoming more reserved and standoffish and he spent a lot of time downstairs in AJ's bedroom. He said it was peaceful for him there and a way to get away from the now crowding family members who came from all over. He would go missing for hours, I totally understood because of the special bond between a father and a son.

# Father Son Duos

Anthony Sr., Tony, and Anthony Jr., AJ.

It was the cutest thing to see the two so close. My husband had a son that was his prize passion some would say. It was always AJ this or AJ that, he's a boy so he needs this unlike the girls. Tony parenting each child like they were the only child, although there were three of them. You could tell Danielle was a typical firstborn, spoiled and selfish. AJ was the first boy and brat and little Lanyia was the baby and that title still remains.

My husband loves his children like

no man I have ever seen before. He's firm but at the same time laid-back and pretty funny at times. I guess that's the Gemini in him.

He would say to me, "Baby, you can't be friends with these kids."

But often, I hear him tell AJ, "You're my best friend boy," and it showed from birth. Tony would take AJ with him anywhere. Two pull ups in his back pocket and a sippy cup was all he needed for Daddy Day Care. Right before AJ was school-age, Tony will let him go everywhere with him, even to work, he tried that 'take your child to work' thing one too many times.

But after he was told that TARC

didn't allow your child to ride the bus all day with him, that ended their Batman and Robin rides.

After that, it was just hard for them to park each day. AJ knew when it was time for Daddy to go to work he would run to him and my husband would say, "I'll see you later man."

AJ would reply, "I love you Daddy" and hug him tight wrapping his little body around Tony's leg. I know he had to be strong in front of him then and had to be even stronger he thought for all of us. I can only imagine what he was down there reminiscing over. This was a loss I couldn't even replace. I wanted to go to him but I just couldn't go down to

AJ's room yet, so I called for him to come upstairs. It was time to go to the viewing.

# The Final Rest

Most of the immediate family met at the funeral home to finally lay eyes on the child I felt was being kept away from us until the ransom that was requested had been paid.

It had been 6 long days without seeing his face & hearing his voice. To us, literally dreading the fact that it was time for us to reunite, but under so many different situations.

The staff at the funeral home tried their very best to prepare us for what was to come next.

I remember the music they were playing in the background as they walked us closely to the casket. I even remember the seats that were behind me that caught my brother's fall. His knees buckled from the site of his nephew being in that casket. We were all living the first moments of our new normal simultaneously.

We all had a reaction, but somehow mine was the one that caused the worst response. I stood over that casket and a beastly motherly roar that had no words, just sound was released out of me with all the pain, hurt and anger.

At its peak, I let it go so loud I know all of city heard my porch call. You know the one we use to get when the streetlights came on and you weren't where you were supposed to be? (at home) That one! This wasn't where my child was supposed to be. He was supposed to still be here with me!!!!

I broke all the way down.

I couldn't think it away anymore. It's him. It's my baby boy! It's really AJ and he's laying here in this casket lifeless.

I heard one of the attendees burst into tears excusing herself from the room. I'm guessing my energy attached itself to her emotional outlet. I couldn't look away. They wanted me to have a seat, but I couldn't leave his side. I just kept saying how sorry I was that I couldn't be there for him and how I'd never forget him and repeated it over and over. "Why didn't you just come with us? Ohhhhhh AJ!"

I had every emotion. Guilt, pain, frustration, blame, emptiness, hopelessness, disappointment and anger. My most important role in life as mother had been reconfigured. I went from 2 biological children to just having one in a week's time. I was undone. I wanted to just stay there with him overnight. Of course, that wasn't an option. We all left, and I couldn't recover from my truth. I didn't care about Valentine's day or nothing else. I just wanted my baby back.

# Heartbroken

I remember that before all this happened, I was planning our church's Couples Retreat / Getaway, which was now being canceled due to his sudden death. I thought about everything I have put together for the couples to rekindle their flickering flames. I had been working on the perfect Retreat for us, planning and purchasing stuff just to be forced to abort that mission.

Now planning to bury my first true love right around this lover's weekend. I didn't have it in me to celebrate. I remember a few weeks prior, AJ asked me, "Mom, are you still going to make me one of those baskets for me and my girlfriend?"

I remember snatching my adult novelties from him and telling him he must be out of his mind.

I told him, "Boy you ain't grown yet! You're getting the same Valentine basket and candy that I gave you every year."

He laughed, kissed me on my cheek and said, "Cool, cool."

He notices the U of L and U of K drinking cups I had pulled out of the bag. He said, "Well Mom, can I least get one of them?"

I took the cup out of his hand and said, "Boy, we will see. Now, see you later AJ."

He left, and I never noticed until that moment that the U of L cup was still sitting on my dresser as if it was my reminder that he wanted that exact one. I went over to it and hugged the cup as if it was full of life. My baby wanted that cup and now he never gets it.

Everyone knew that our AJ knew how much he loved the Louisville Cardinals. Right in that thought, I decided to make the announcement that we will all be wearing red and white or Louisville sports gear to his home-going celebration. This had been one of the most pressing issues on my mind.

# The Die Hard Cardinal Fan

What did he want to wear? He's not an everyday suit person and nothing traditional fit this occasion. My son walked out the back door in sweats, Jordans and a Louisville t-shirt in hopes of coming right back home. Well, he didn't make it back to our house, but at least we could send him home feeling like himself.

I had dressed him up all his life for baby pictures, family pictures, Easter, etc. But this time, I'll let my son have his day like he would have wanted. Surrounding him with loyal friends and close family with a nice song or two and plenty of food. The day had to be perfectly AJ.

That night, I got some much needed rest. I felt like AJ would be proud of his mom and dad and how even though during the roughest time in our life and marriage, we stuck together for better or for worse. Somehow, honoring God, our vows and him all at the same time.

# Rain Sleet or Snow, We Gotta Go

That night the weather got bad. It was a winter snow storm almost blizzard like. We were afraid of being told that the roads were too bad, and we may have to postpone or cancel the funeral service until the weather cleared.

Our phone started ringing early. People were worried that the weather would keep them from attending. I had never heard of canceling a funeral service before, but I thought it was kind of like the motto, rain, sleet or snow it's happening.

I called the funeral home and they

answer, "Yes ma'am. We have already taken his body to the church, and we have plans to proceed."

For a second, I thought we were off the hook for the day, but nevertheless, we had to be there. We did but the now popular same day service where the wake and the funeral were held together. I couldn't imagine a two-day event.

The day of the service seemed like it was flying by. It was time for us to leave for the service. I remember the prescription that I had filled that the doctor prescribed, just in case I needed something to help me cope with the next few weeks. I put them in my purse, just in case!

We arrived at the church this time before the service started. I couldn't sit through the wake. My nerves were shot from thinking that nobody will be able to attend, but as we made it up to the parking lot, it was full.

Cars fully covered the lot. We walked into hundreds of people. I couldn't believe my eyes. God did It again!

# Love Conquers All

As far as my eyes could see, there was red and white carnations all in the sanctuary. Wow! AJ would have been really pleased.

Everybody came out and showed their love and payed their respects. It was beautiful. The singing, the poems and the eulogy. Even more souls were baptized. Ending the service, was the hardest part knowing that this was our final farewell. No more earthly visits.

# Wait

Rewinding my mind's DVD player pausing into slow motion, I can see the funeral director lowering the casket after removing AJ's beloved Beats, and his Instagram famous gold iced out watch, which was the first piece of jewelry he bought for himself, being removed from his arm.

That took Lanyia out! Seeing that casket closing in the end of the final chapter of his life. I recognized Nyia hadn't said much about anything during this whole ordeal. She shed a tear here and there and then would leave the room. Well not this time. AJ was leaving the room. The person at the top of everybody's conversation, who typically caused her to want to leave the room, was not only exiting the room, but from her whole life. Her first friend, her big brother, her sibling overseer, the one who taught her so much, even how to cover for him. Their relationship was ending, and he was gone from her life.

In that moment, as their mother, I saw that the girls both lost a best friend, their body guard and a brother all-in-one. I couldn't do enough to console either one of them but Nyia and I both needed help and had to have ushers help us walk behind the casket. I ran down the center aisle and held onto the rolling casket. It was my last attempt to fight with death and just maybe, I could have wake him from this deep slumber. I was given water as if it would quench the thirst for my child that it was craving.

The family huddled around me, caressing and praying for me, distracting me from the atmosphere long enough to help the funeral home workers escort his body to the hearse. We didn't have a repass because he was being cremated.

He went back with them and I

had to stay and play nice with our company. All I wanted to do was leave and go far away from life as I once lived it.

# He Was Here

In three weeks, we were supposed to be celebrating AJ's 19th birthday. How does one celebrate the life of a person twice in the same month, holding in one hand a birth certificate and a death certificate in the other? I was back to being emotionally exhausted.

I now had my weight, Tony's, Lanyia's, Danielle's, my mother's, and brother's weight all on my shoulders. Not to mention, the rest of the family and his many friends too. All the little kids that love Uncle and cousin AJ. It began to be too much on them all. I have poured myself out empty. I didn't have a drop of empathy left to offer.

I remember sitting in the living room waiting for my friend to pick me up. She came over nearly every day to get me out of the house. She knew I hated being alone with all my emotions. As I waited for her, I noticed the hospice information and number on a pad on the coffee table. I took out my phone and dialed the number thinking they said they could help. I received the voicemail center. I left my name and number and then dismissed the whole thing.

I was caught off-guard with the call back that same day.

"Hello, Elgina. I see that you called. Can we set you up with an appointment?"

I replied, "Ok." Not quite sure what I was signing up for.

"I have an opening this week on Wednesday at 2:00."

I confirmed that was fine. She also after ask me a few more questions, stated they would even have a counselor stop by and visit Lanyia at school. She explained that the entire immediate family could sit in group sessions that are held during the week. Accepting the help was one of the best ideas we could have agreed on.

# We Need To Talk

We had serious topics that needed professional attention. We decided to have AJ cremated and this was a complete first for our entire family. Some were even upset with our decision, but it was our best choice. Not knowing what happened to him or who did it made me uneasy, thinking he wouldn't get his proper rest even after death. People, strangers and foes could have free access to our son.

Even the thoughts of bad weather hindering us from visiting him on his birthday or the holidays I just couldn't bear. God forbid if we moved out of state. I wanted what I could have of our child to remain with us at least for the rest of my life.

The meeting with the counselor was so important because just having a non-biased person that listened and didn't judge was so refreshing. We were giving our first glance at hope that we were fit to live with this new normal life. We were told about a sudden loss in homicide program in a memorial service that was held in March every year. I was like no way, like this event was happening days before his 19th birthday. I knew we had to attend, if I didn't know anything else, my family will be there. I remember our entire support system being so grateful to learn that there was still loving good-hearted people remaining in this world, that truly have a passion for understanding the pain of other mourning people. No matter what happened to the deceased or loved one.

# In Your Honor

Being that it was 9 days before his birthday, it just felt right and really wonderful being around other people that life happened to. Seeing and hearing about them doing the work to relive again this time with the sole purpose of keeping their loved one's memory alive. I prayed that right there in my seat one day, I too, would return with my true story. That I'm a living witness for this new normal life that I'm breathing through with AJ as my new exhaling inspiration! He would now live through me! Somehow that gave me a rebirthing experience.

Over the next few months on this journey will mirror a pregnancy. The same way people felt about the news of a new baby they're happy for you. On the other hand, learning of the passing death of AJ, people were sad for me and through the next few months, I'd be questioned about the loss of my child.

Like any pregnant mother is about her due date, the closer to AJ's birthday, just like with an expecting mother, she has a baby shower for her newly-born child. I wanted to have a birthday celebration for my absent deceased son. We both know the sex and birth date and all the things we like to have for our baby. It's just that mine will only be for memory sake while hers will be used to create memories.

I told myself I still wanted to celebrate my child that was here for 18 years, 11 months, and three days, so my family honored my wishes in every way possible.

# Never Forgotten

We never leave AJ out of any family events or special occasions, and he even sends us gifts from heaven. I remember the first Christmas without him. I didn't think we could do it because the year before was his last and best Christmas since the drum set.

We had had an amazing holiday weekend. And not to mention it was so pressing on my heart for some reason to do a huge Christmas that year with plenty of gifts. Everyone had a good Christmas, especially AJ. He got everything on his list. The smile on his face was and remains priceless as I remember how he danced, hugged, and kissed us. Boy, we were so happy.

To go from Christmas 2014 with him to Christmas 2015 without him, we needed a lifeline, so I prayed and asked for a sign and heaven answered. The family receive Christmas gifts from AJ from heaven. It took some work, but by the grace of God it turned out to be one of the most amazing Christmas memories ever.

Everyone was grateful and cherished their gifts. Especially the men in the family who had been holding it together by a thin thread, trying to stay strong for us. I made sure to personally pick gifts that would speak to the heart of the brokenness and masculinity and at the same time being symbolic to the relationship with AJ. The response was overwhelming. They all released with tears and cleansing conversations about him as if the presents made him present. They thanked AJ and made promises to stay strong and play this game of life out to the fullest. It was so rewarding to capture this memory and make it a part of our new normal. I believe nothing will ever make a mourner whole again after the loss of a loved one, but you can live again if you really try.

My daily mission is to find ways and outlets to heal and draw the broken pieces of my heart back together. By sharing my truth with others, we have attended grief camp and many other family healing sessions. Believe me, it all helps. However, being that we are made up of mind, body, and spirit, I've explored every avenue. I truly believe there's more than just one source of healing and for me, I needed the best available plan that helped the whole person.

I have found that there are so many outlets to pull good energy from. Let's face it, there's really no good grief, but good can really come out of the grief but you have to go through it.

It's been a few years now, and I can truly say the first year everything was extremely hard. The second year was not too much better, but this third, fourth, and fifth year, I have been able to thank God for all the people, places, and information I received over this Faith walk that I now have to hold onto and reference back to in my time of crisis.

I have shared my proof with hundreds of people over this short time frame. I even went back and spoke at a Hope and Healing Festival in honor of my son like I promised myself right before his 21st birthday. It was amazing to tell my truth to mothers that sit in that room looking for Hope as I once did. I now host grief seminars aiding and assisting mourning mothers.

I help with everything from

planning the funeral to shopping for final requests or using my cosmetology license, styling hair for the deceased and their loved ones. My thoughts are, "that someone did it for me in my time of need." There's nothing else I sincerely desire but to be of assistance. I just want to be a blessing by easing the load off of a mourning mother just like good people did for me and my family. AJ continues to live everyday through me and my sincere acts of kindness.

I have hopes of one day opening several Anthony group home centers for at-risk boys and girls who suffer from homelessness. There they will be provided with plenty of love, life skills, and the Lord as if they were my own.

I plan to have a house near every school to ensure their ability to be present and active. I believe everything happens for a reason, and my reason for living and not to give up and dying happens to be for the same person. His death has taught me to live in the moment, be present with the family you have left, and to make memories with what turns into legacies.

I'm relearning to enjoy life and to stop wishing the time that I have here on Earth away. I really see that I'm needed here and that there's work for me to get done. You know we all have a purpose. When it's the end of your stay here on Earth, what will be said about what you did in between your birth and departure? I can honestly say that my child touched the lives of many and through his life and death, I found the light even though the darkest of days that will one day lead me back to him.

My angel guides me through this journey and continue sending me signs to let me know he's near. I'm known as the bird watcher because I can spot a Redbird a mile away. I see life differently and enjoy nature in the simple things like family night. It's no longer important to work more than I have to. I'd rather budget tighter than spend my time away from my family.

We now take several yearly vacations to create new memories and yes, will do bring AJ along. We have promised each other to love with all we have to offer, give everything we have to give to one another, and leave this world empty knowing we used up everything we had in us to share, with helping someone like us. As mourners, we each have a separate assignment that collectively connects to purpose.

# Good Grief

This took me a long time to say, but my truth is you and your family can live this new normal life if you all take it one day at a time! Don't be guilted into not living, because your loved one is living through you. Don't die on them before your time. Remain hopeful that there will be a brighter morning that will appear after mourning.

Conclusion: Heavenly Father, I know every human being suffers through struggles, setbacks, and disappointments. Lord knows since the beginning; mankind has suffered through trouble times. This will continue until you return to establish the eternal peace.

Through me reading and studying the Bible, God has given me a message of hope, reassurance, and encourages me to persevere knowing that he watches over us and he is with us at all times. Rest in the author of your faith, Jesus Christ.

Here are some passages to inspire and give you comfort through those difficult times when you have questions and no answers.

**Let go and Let God**

Psalm 55:22, "Give your burdens to the Lord, and He will take care of you. He will not permit the godly to slip and fall."

**Don't worry and Find Peace of Mind**

Philippians 4: 6-7, "Don't worry about anything; instead, pray about everything. Tell God what you need and thank him for all he has done. then you will experience God's peace, which exceeds anything we can understand. His peace will guard your hearts and minds as you live in Christ Jesus."

## God Understands Our Pain and Anguish

Psalm 34:18, "The Lord is near to the brokenhearted and saves the crushed in spirit."

## Through God, All can be Overcome

Isaiah 40:28-31, "He gives power to the weak and strength to the powerless, but those who trust in the Lord will find new strength."

## God is Always With Us

Deuteronomy 32:8, "It is the Lord who goes before you. He will be with you; he will not leave you or forsake you. Do not fear or be dismayed."

## We Have Nothing to Fear, even death

Psalm 23:4, "Even though I walk through the valley of the shadow of death, I fear no evil, for You are with me; Your rod and Your staff, they comfort me."

## God Sends the Holy Spirit and Jesus to Give Us Comfort and Peace

John 14:26-27, "Jesus said, But the comforter, the Holy Spirit, whom the father will send in my name, will teach you all things and will remind you of everything I have told you. Peace I leave with you; my peace I give you. I do not give to you as the world gives. Do not let your hearts be troubled and do not be afraid."

I've asked myself a thousand times throughout this entire process does it really matter the who or the why regarding my son's death? It's been a hard mental debate. Honestly, neither can undo what's been done and allowed.

I'm reminded with hope, John 3:16, "For God so loved the world that He gave His one and only son, that whoever believes in Him shall not perish, but have eternal life." (NKJV)

So, by me letting go of the torment and trusting God with the truth, freeze my heart, mind, and spirit to be loved by the father that created me and has permission to orchestrate every area of my life, good, bad, happy or sad.

He's the Author and Finisher of my faith, Romans 8:38-39, King James Version.

38 For I am persuaded, that neither death, nor life, nor angels, nor principalities, nor powers, nor things present, nor things to come,

39 Nor height, nor depth, nor any other creature, shall be able to separate us from the love of God, which is in Christ Jesus our lord.

May God bless you all on this new normal journey and keep you in his perfect peace. Amen

Elgina.

# Acknowledgements

To Our girls, Danielle and La'nyia, thank you both for never giving up on us. Thanks for supporting us through all the first we struggled through without your brother, our AJ. You two have experienced a great loss that no siblings should ever have to endure. You two are your brother's keeper and you've helped to keep his memories alive in so many ways. We love you ladies dearly and may God continue to mend our brokenness while drawing us closer to him and one another.

We never would've made it through without you, Jeanine Lee, my mother, the late Phyllis Smith, Anthony's mother. The late Elgin Bullock, my father and Emmit Smith and his family, Anthony's father.

The late Ann Levette Smith,

Anthony's sister, my brother, Elgin Bullock Jr and his family. My sisters, Stephanie Lee and Jasmine Lee. My half-brothers, Cameron Bullock and Justin Bullock.

My entire Bullock and Badon family. Special thanks to Terrance Bullock and Kenny Badon. My grandmother, Julie Grice and to my Suggs and Nixon family.

All my mother's sisters and brothers, and the entire Williams family, I love every one of you! My Smith's and Grove's family.

To our bonus family, Nicola Warr and family, Dana Jenkins and her son, and Lu'wena Ingram.

My best friend Tinika and Morris Rinehardt - AJ and La'nyia's godparents
Denise & Billy Neal – My godparents
Best friend, Kecia Sloss

Alisha Nelson
Fa'lesha Pitts
LaMesa Marks-John
Lennett and Lenell Martin
Steve and Tanita Thompson
Dresean Scotland and family
Nicole Watson
Jacoby Osborne
Tyron Morris
Nate
Walter
Aale'jah King

Wanda and Michael Holt, you all have been a daily blessing and a remaining support system for our family we love you dearly.

Our sincerest thanks go to Bishop William Harris and First Lady Regena Harris, you two held our hand and walked us through a very dark season in our life. We are better today because you both helped us through. (Praise Covenant Church Louisville)
Special honor to Elder Jorge and

Janine Sanchez. Elder Clayton and Dr.
Lisa Robertson and Perry and Chrystel
Blair.

To our Support Group:
The Robinsons
The Combs
The Archies
The Fourtneys
Felica Manley
Mother Brown and her family,
And each and every member of Praise
Covenant Church that loved on us
through those dark days.

Thank you to all my industry family,
Savina, Savina's top notch salon
Jason Wyatt
Shantia Bibbs
Lisa Wilson
Cedric Wages
Bert Fitzgerald
Mimi Kidd
Courtney People
Mariyon Thomas-Brown
Belinda Billingsley

Stacey Shivley
Jennifer Renfro
Kristey Hardison
Denise Beasley

All of Anthony's TARC family

My Prayer Warrior Circle:
Pastor Janeen Drake
Elder Jeanine Lee
Pastor Susan Bradley
Rev. Yvonne McCoy-Oasis
Pastor Artrice Hansberry
Nakkia Bowen
First Lady Patricia Nixon
Jacklyn Walker.

Last but not least, Iisha Bullock, my sister in love. Thank you for everything Sissy you held me up when I absolutely couldn't with all the heavy loads, you helped me bare. I'm forever grateful, I love you.

Everyone from my mourning mother group.

Thank you, thank you, thank you, to all my clients that remained loyal and allowed me the much needed time to grieve,

Special thanks to:
Main One Financial
Hathaway and Clark Funeral Home
Hospice – the hope and healing staff
Angie Higdon
Western High School staff and students class of 2011-2015

One of the biggest thanks goes to Mrs. Julia Royston, CEO and owner of BK Royston Publishing Company

And now I want to thank you, the reader for picking my book out of all the books that you had to select from you made my story your choice.

As you're turning the pages of my life's truth, I pray that something you read helps you along your journey as well.

God bless you,

Elgina Bullock-Smith

Made in the USA
Monee, IL
18 July 2023

39379889R00121